U Janal Aj Maya

Traditional Maya Cuisine

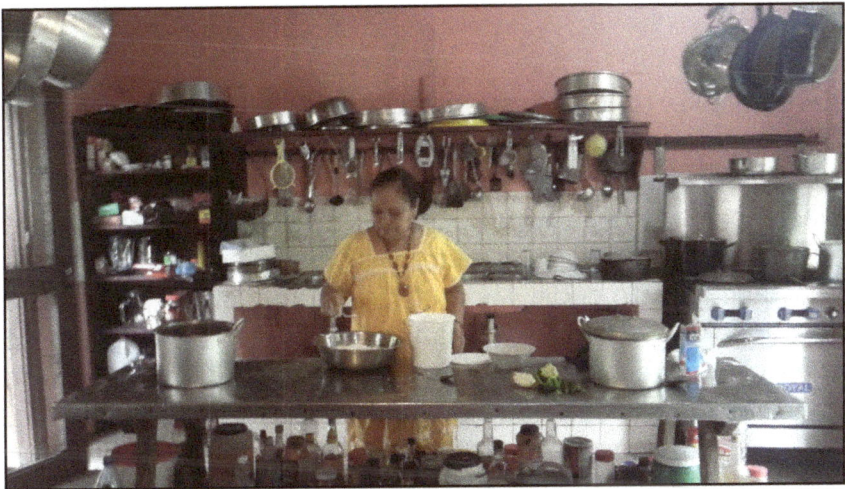

Acknowledgements

Yucatec Maya:

Bele tin tza'jic a Dios Botic ti tulacalex a wanta jenex in metic' ej' joon, elela ete in wili, Juana Saqui toop qi u men jana, ix Amy Lichty, Dorothy Beveridge, Judy Lumb, ix voluun tubi teen u gabajoo. Ti in tat Aurelio Garcia icjkool winic, y lete ti tan ej jau'oo, ku metic' yaba jana' too'n. Ti in na ix Paulina Mex, letie'j too'p qi u jana sian, y tin walic' botic' ti talacal ti nola y ti noloo' tux ca'ansajoon ik jana yokol ku' paj'talic wesic' ti u lack mac' y ti tulacal yok'ol cab, Bele'j Dios Botic tex.

Mopan Maya:

In c'ati in tza botik ti tulacale'ex. A wantajene'esx in mete aj juunai, ti in wili'i ix Juana Saki toop ki u janal, ti in amiga ix Amy Lichty, Dorothy Beveridge, y Judy Lumb ti ej tzuputalo ti anta (ix volunteers) tubi ten u c'abaoo'. Ti in tat Aurelio Garcia, juntul aj qui'ecj pan winik. Le'ec ti tan a ja'aj, walac u caal ti men janal to'on. In na ix Paulina Mesj, to'op qui' u janal men tac wejej. Ti tulacal ti na'cjinoo' ti tataoo' u ca'ansajoono ti men janal ti'i toon yoc'laal ma ti tubsic. Yoc'laal ti'i caj yej a labe ti'i tulac' mac' y tula cal yoc'ol cab. Botic teje'ex.

English:

I would like to thank everybody that helped me put this book together, including my mother-in-law Juana Saqui, Amy Lichty, Dorothy Beveridge, Judy Lumb, and all the volunteers whose names I have forgotten. My father Aurelio Garcia is a special dad. He was a farmer. On rainy days he stayed home and taught us to cook. My mother, Paulina Mesh, also was a great cook. I would like to thank all my ancestors that passed the knowledge of cooking on to their children so that we can share it with you all now and to the world. Thank you.

U Janal
Aj Maya

Traditional Maya Cuisine

Aurora Garcia Saqui
with Amy Lichty

Producciones de la Hamaca
Caye Caulker, BELIZE
2013

photos curtesy of Dorothy Beveridge, Amy E. Lichty,
        Judy Lumb and Eurnesto Saqui

Published by *Producciones de la Hamaca*
Caye Caulker, BELIZE
<producciones-hamaca.com>

ISBN: 978-976-8142-54-2

Producciones de la Hamaca is dedicated to:
- Celebration and documentation of Belize's rich, diverse cultural heritage,
  - Protection and sustainable use of Belize's remarkable natural resources,
   - Inspired, creative expression of Belize's spiritual depth.

Table of Contents

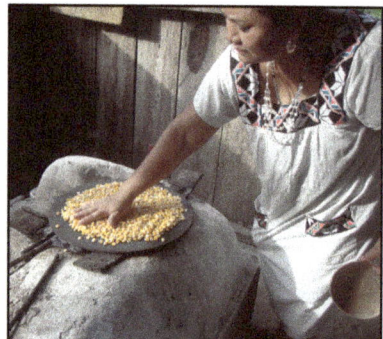

Introduction

The Mayan ancestors obtained their food from the forest and plants that had been domesticated for thousands of years. Corn (maize) was the main staple of the Mayan empire. When there was a drought and the corn harvest didn't produce the needed food supply, fruit of the breadnut tree was often harvested.

corn field

I am a Yucatec Maya who grew up in San Antonio, Cayo District, Belize. My mother told us a story from when she was a child. One year the corn crop didn't do well because of drought, but my grandfather planted his corn at the right time and the harvest was productive. The villagers came to my grandfather and traded gold coins for ears of corn. While gold was valuable, there wasn't much that it could be traded for, so he buried it like you would put money in a bank. Through stories passed down the generations, we know that the Ancient Maya planted Ceiba trees to mark where they had buried their treasures. To this day, my grandfather's gold is still hidden away and may very well be at the base of a Ceiba tree.

The atole is a special drink of the Maya made from corn. My medicine teacher and great uncle, Don Elijio Panti, drank atole every morning and lived to 110 years of age. We know that when we eat natural plants that are free of pesticides and animals that haven't been given hormones or antibiotics, we are caring for our physical well-being. When we cook the meals of our ancestors, we are giving honour to their wisdom and at the same time, feeding our spiritual well-being.

In Maya ceremonies that thank the gods and honour the ancestors, corn is very important. Pah Sa is a special drink made with fermented blue corn that we make for our deceased ancestors. The Bix ceremony is performed on the second of November. In the morning the offering includes only bread and the cocoa drink, and in the evening the table is set with all of the ancestors' favorite foods and drink. The table is set with a candle on each corner to give light to the ancestors, and it is said that when the ceremony is over, the ancestors take the light with them to guide them on their journey.

Ernesto Saqui saying prayers to the corn god

My father practiced Si'ioolal ceremony when he harvested his corn. He picked the best six ears of green corn, set them in the middle of the house on a table, along with four white candles, and said his prayers to the corn god, Yum Kaax, giving thanks for an abundant harvest. The rain god, Chac, was called upon and given thanks for providing much needed water. My father also evoked the other spirits, such as the gods of the birds, animals, and insects because they did not harm the crop before it was harvested.

When I was nine, my mother told me it was time to learn how to cook. In the Maya culture females are responsible for the cooking in the home. She was showing me how to cook so I would be prepared to cook for my future family. When I was ready to learn how to make tortillas, my father went into the jungle to get a wo' frog. The wo' frog is black with white stripes and only comes out in the beginning of the rainy season during the heavy rains. He gave me the frog and told me to rub it between my hands, back and forth, nine times. Learning how to stroke the frog would help me to make a perfect tortilla that would puff up like the belly of the frog!

After I married, I learned how to prepare the dishes of the Mopan Maya from my mother-in-law. Over the course of a year, we lived with my husband's parents and I helped prepare all the meals. What was different from my mother's cooking was the variety of soups I learned to make and some of those recipes are in this cookbook.

Aurora Saqui with fresh limes

This cookbook contains those recipes that have been passed down through the generations. I have been serving them to visitors for years. They always ask me how I can cook such delicious food and I answer, "Because I cook with love." We all know how easy it is to go out to eat in a restaurant, but nothing is better than a home-cooked meal that is wonderfully flavored with native plants, and served with love.

The Garden

In Belize we cook using plants that are in season using vegetables and fruits that are native to the region or grown here rather than imported. Some local crops have the same English name, but they are a different variety than that used abroad, such as corn, oregano, pumpkin, and yam.

Allspice—The ground dried friut is used for seasoning. The fruit is picked when green and dried in the sun.

Annatto—The reddish coating of the annatto (achiote) seeds is extracted and used for giving colour and adding a unique flavor. Annatto is available in the Punta Gorda market but can be difficult to get elsewhere. If you substitute red recado, it will have a different flavor but it will still be tasty.

Banana—The banana leaf is used as a wrap to contain ingredients and impart a unique flavor. Waha leaf can be used in place of a banana leaf to wrap and cook fish. Outside of Central America you might use aluminum foil.

Calalloo—This nutritious plant grows wild or can be planted. It was a source of food for the ancient Maya. It can be boiled or the raw leaves can be used in a salad. Similar greens such as chaya and spinach can be used as substitutes.

Chocho—The fruit of the chocho (wiskill, chayote) vine is used in soups or as a flavoring. Pumpkin has a similar flavor and can be used as a substitute.

Chaya—The ancient Maya domesticated chaya from the wild. The leaves can be cooked, eaten raw, or made into a juice.

Cilantro—This herb is used for flavoring for any food, especially soups. It does not grow wild in Belize, so it must be planted.

Coco—The root of the coco (cocoyam, elephant ear, taro) plant can be used as a potato. It has a similar flavor, but a velvety texture that holds together in a soup or stew. Yam is a good substitute for coco because it doesn't alter the flavor of the recipe.

annatto pods

annatto seeds

banana leaves

chaya

calalloo

cilantto

coco

coco root

Cohune Palm—The nuts of this rainforest palm are harvested to make oil. Coconut and other vegetable oils can be substituted, but they will have different flavors. The cohune heart of palm is the top center of a young tree trunk and is used as food.

Corn—The main staple of the Mayan empire, corn (maize) has been domesticated for thousands of years. When the corn is properly dried in the field, it is harvested. The ears of corn are cut off the stalk and bagged for storage. The corn can also be stored in a stack box called a "troja" where the ears are layered until they reach the beam of the house. The dry corn will last for a long time. It is ground before use as food, as in masa, atole, and porridge. This corn of the Maya is not the same as sweet corn in North America, but more similar to what is called "field corn" or "Indian corn" in North America.

The dry corn husk is moistened prior to being used as a wrap.

Green or young corn is picked before it dries and used for making porridge or tamalitos.

Culantro—A perennial herb used for seasoning soups and salads. Culantro grows along roadsides, in old fields, and in yards. Cilantro, which is similar in flavor, can be used as a substitute.

Jipijapa—This plant, native to the southern part of Belize, is most well known as materials for weaving baskets, but parts of it are eaten. The young shoots that emerge at the same time as the new moon are edible. Bamboo shoots can be used as a substitute because they have a similar consistency and flavor. The leaves from the young shoots are separated, torn in half lengthwise, and used to tie wrapped foods such as tamales. The jipijapa pods appear around the full moon. Before they open, the hairy flower inside the immature pod is edible. When the pod opens, it reveals a red interior with black seeds that can be planted.

Lime—The juice of the lime is used to wash meat, to flavor many recipes, and is made into a drink.

cohune palm

corn

culantro

dry corn

jipijapa

pulling

jipijapi young shoot

lime

obel

Obel—The obel (cow's foot) leaves have an anise flavor and are used as a seasoning. Basil can be substituted for obel, but it doesn't have the anise flavor.

Okra—This plant is used in soups or as a side dish.

Onion—Green onion leaves are used as flavoring. Chives can be substituted.

Oregano—There are two different oregano plants growing in gardens, one with thick leaves, which is cut finely for use, and the other with thin leaves that can be used dried or green. Commercial oregano, which is a different plant, can be used as a substitute.

Peppers—There are several varieties of hot spicy peppers, such as, habanero, jalapeño, and bird peppers.

Plantain—Also called "cooking bananas", plantains are a staple in the Maya diet.

Pumpkin—A type of squash used in soups and as a vegetable. It is not the North American Halloween pumpkin.

Recado—Red recado is made from ground annatto (achiote) seeds with spices added. Black recado is made from charred hot peppers instead of annatto. Red and black recado are available in ethnic grocery stores.

Squash—One of the more popular squashes grown in Belize is the variety used in this cookbook.

Sweet Potato—The most common sweet potato in Belize is dark red on the outside and light yellow inside, but there are two other varieties, one white and one yellow. None is the same as what is called "sweet potato" in North America. Sweet potatoes are cooked in a variety of ways and served as a side dish, but they are not used in soups.

Yam—This root crop has several varieties, all of which are brown outside and white inside. Yams are used in making soups. None is the same as the yam used in North America.

Waha—The large leaf of this plant can be used to wrap ingredients if no banana leaves are available.

bird peppers

oregano, thick leaves

plantain

pumpkin

okra

squash

sweet ppotato

waha leaf

Aurora in garden
showing waha

recado paste

The Maya Kitchen

In addition to pots, pans, measuring spoons, cups, knives, and utensils, the following are used in the Maya kitchen:

Fire hearth—A cooking area made from clay and ashes that is painted either with white lime or red clay. A stove or barbeque can be substituted depending on the recipe.

Comal—The comal is Maya cooking surface that is round and flat. The traditional comal is made of clay and fired, but today most use iron comals that are available from the Mennonites. A griddle or frying pan can be substituted.

Fry Pan—A cast iron skillet used for frying or cooking food on a fire hearth or stove.

Hand Mill—A hand grinder used for grinding grains. In Belize a hand mill can be purchased at a hardware store. An electric grinder or food processor can be substituted.

Masher—A metal tool used for mashing food by hand.

Matate—A large flat stone surface with stone rolling pin to crush leaves. A rolling pin could be substituted.

Mortar and Pestle—A small deep bowl and grinder made of rock that is used for crushing herbs and spices.

Strainer—A calabash gourd is drilled with holes about an inch apart. It is used when washing corn to separate the skin from the kernel. A strainer basket of a spaghetti pot or a colander with large holes can be substituted.

Tortilla Press—A quality press will be made of cast iron; the plates are heavy and require less force to get an even press to shape tortillas. To care for your press, simply wipe it clean.

Maya kitchen

white lime

fire hearth

cooking on fire hearth

comal

fry pan

masher

mortar & pestle

hand mill

strainer

matate

tortilla press

White Lime—White lime is used to soak the corn overnight when making masa. White lime can be purchased at a farm center where seeds and implements are sold. Traditionally white lime is made by putting limestone on top of a wood pile and burning overnight. Freshwater snail shells (jute) can also be used, but the burning only takes half a day because they are smaller. Water is then thrown on the ashes until the chunks all explode into a powder. Gumbo limbo wood is preferred because using white lime burned with gumbo limbo firewood to make masa helps to preserve the cooked corn for a longer period of time.

The men of the family make the white lime and they make enough for a whole year at once. More than one family might work together. They burn it during the dry season in their milpa because they don't want the fire to get wet. White lime is very important to the Mayan culture because without it our corn tortillas cannot be made.

Preparations

Wash vegetables and herbs in water only. Wash meat in water with vinegar or lime juice unless it is being used for a soup or stew. Meat for soup or stew is washed in boiling water.

If you are not in Central America, you may not find all the ingredients, so possible substitutions for ingredients are in the Garden section (p. 4). Substitutions for kitchen equipment can be found in the descriptions of the Maya Kitchen (p. 10).

The recipes in this book are listed by their Yucatec Maya name. The other names may include Mopan Maya (M), Creole (C), Spanish (S), or English (E).

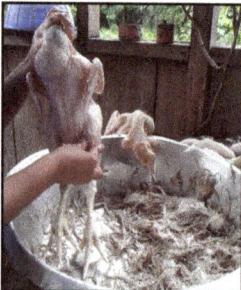

| chicken | plucking feathers | searing feathers |

Prepared Ingredients

C'uxub
Annatto (S)

Makes one small bottle

    8 lbs annatto seeds
    3 gal water

To extract the red colouring from the seeds, soak them for two days in two gallons of water. Wash the seeds with your hands in the soaking pot until the seeds turn white. Strain the entire mixture into another pot. Rinse the seeds with an additional gallon of water and strain into the pot. Throw away the seeds. Cook the mixture in the pot on low heat for three days, stirring once in a while, until it forms a red paste. Cool and bottle. This will keep for about a year at room temperature when stored in a cool location. Use for red food colouring. One pinch will go a long way.

Tuzt
Cohune Palm Oil (E)

Makes 1 quart oil

    8 lbs cohune nuts, shelled
    water

Collect cohune nuts in the dry season because they have the most oil. Crack open the cohune nuts with a large rock or the back of an axe. It might take about two days to crack enough nuts to get eight pounds of kernels. Grind the kernels in a large wooden mortar, about three feet tall, called "pilon." Add to a large pot of boiling water. Boil on high heat for 24 hours, keeping the pot full of water. Set overnight to cool, and then scrape off the oil floating on the top. Boil the collected oil to remove any remaining water for about 30 minutes. Leave to cool and bottle.

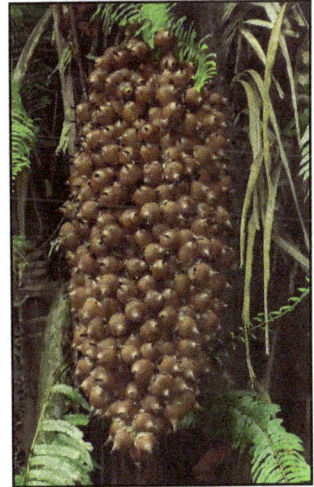

cohune nuts

Su'can
Masa (S), Corn Dough (E)

Makes 5 lbs of dough

1 lb dried corn (yellow or white)
½ C white lime
1 gal water

Shell the dry corn. Wash the white lime and add the wash water into a pot. Add the shelled corn to the pot, not more than half of the pot because it will swell. Throw away any trash floating on top. Heat until the water begins to boil. Lower the heat and test every now and again until you

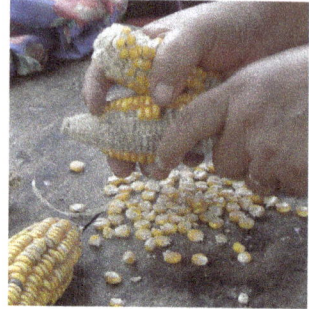

shelling dry corn

see the corn skin peeling off, about ten minutes. Remove from the heat and leave it overnight. Wash the corn thoroughly to remove the skins. Grind the corn in a hand mill. After grinding, the corn masa is ready to be made into tortillas. Masa harina can be purchased in ethnic grocery stores and used as a substitute for masa.

lighting fire

cooling pot of corn

straning corn

corn skin peeling off

washing corn

corn ready to grind

14

Beverages

Sah'
Atole (S)
Corn Porridge (E)

6 servings

½ lb masa
1 L water
sugar to taste
optional: milk and cinnamon
traditional: black pepper
Q'eq'chi Maya: hot peppers or fresh black beans

Dissolve the masa in one-quarter of the water. Bring the rest of the water to a boil. Add dissolved masa. Stir until it boils. Remove the pot from the fire and keep stirring until it thickens,

dissolving masa

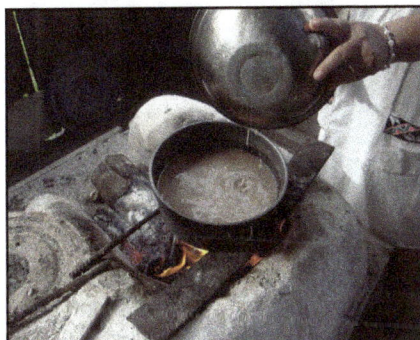
adding dissolved masa

about five minutes. Season to taste and serve hot.

Pah Sah'
2 C black (blue) corn
2 L water

Soak black (blue) corn in one liter water for two days. Rinse the corn and grind. Strain and cook in one liter water until it thickens. Boil for 15 minutes then serve.

This special drink, which is made for the ancestors, is served as an offering during the Bix ceremony which takes place on the second of November.

Ixzim Ca'pe

Corn Coffee (E)

1 lb dry corn (yellow or blue) or old tortillas

Roast the shelled corn on a comal, stirring constantly for about one hour on high heat, until the corn is dark brown and roasted. Grind with a hand mill and store in an airtight container until ready to brew in a coffeemaker. Or, bring a liter of water to boil, add one cup of corn coffee grinds, cover and let set for several minutes.

placing corn on comal

roasting corn

grinding roasted corn

ground roasted corn

cup of ixzim ca'pe

Horchata

20 servings

½ lb rice
1 T cinnamon
1 T nutmeg
¼ lb sugar or to taste
1 gal water

Roast the rice on a comal under very low heat for 15 minutes. Grind in a hand mill or matate very finely. Add cinnamon, nutmeg, and sugar to taste. Mix with one gallon water and serve chilled.

Horchata

Cu'cu U'kul
Cacao Drink (E)

10 servings

½ lb dried cacao beans
2 L boiling water

Roast the dried cacao beans on a grill for 45 minutes over low heat, turning often. Cool and peel the thin skin by hand. Shake in a small basket and blow it so the skin will fly away. Grind in a matate to a fine paste which has lots of oil. Dissolve in boiling water and add flavoring to taste.

cacao beans (tan ones on the left)

Traditional:
black pepper

Optional:
sugar, cinnamon, cloves

17

Breakfast

Ac'p'ac Etel Je'e
Fried Tomatoes with Eggs (E)

4 servings

  1 lb tomatoes, diced
  4 eggs
  1 medium onion, diced
  2 T oil
  salt to taste

Fry the onions in oil until brown, and drop the tomatoes in the skillet, adding salt and stirring constantly for 15 minutes. Then break the eggs and drop in the skillet. Continue stirring until the eggs are cooked. Serve with toast or tortillas.

ac'p'ac etel je'e

Mun Sah'
Green Corn Porridge (E)

Makes 6 cups

  4 ears of green (young) corn
  1 L water
  sugar to taste
  optional: milk

Boil the water. Cut the kernels off the cob, grind in a hand mill and add to the water. Stir until boiling. Lower the heat and keep stirring until it thickens, about five minutes. Add sugar and/or milk and serve.

Que' Yem
Pozole (S) Corn Porridge (E)

Makes 10 cups

2 C of dried corn
1T white lime
4 L water
sugar or honey to taste

For eating: Bring the corn to a boil with white lime in one liter of water, set until the corn skin is peeling off, and wash as for masa (p. 14). Then boil the washed corn in three liters of water until the kernels burst, about one hour. Grind in a hand mill, mix in water, and sweeten with brown sugar or honey to taste.

boiling washed corn

ready to serve

cup of que'yem

For offering: Que' yem is prepared during milpa planting and sweetened with wild honey from the jungle as an offering for the gods. Cook the corn without white lime on high heat in five gallons water until the kernels burst. Strain and grind in a hand mill, skin and all. Mix with one liter of water. Sweeten with wild honey. The offering is set on the milpa site with lit candles. Prayers are said in reverence.

19

Soups

Caldo Caax
Caldo (M) Maya Chicken Soup (E)

4-6 servings

1 medium chicken
1 pinch of annatto
3 cloves garlic, crushed
2 medium chocho, quartered
2 medium coco, cut into bite sizes
1 large onion, sliced
8 leaves fresh culantro
1 handful dried oregano
1½ L water
1 bunch of green onion leaves
salt to taste

tearing culantro

oregano drying

cut up chicken

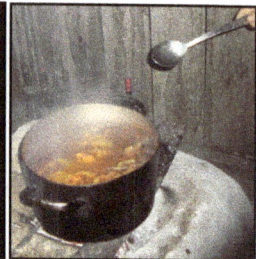

caldo boiling

Cut the chicken into serving pieces, wash in hot water. In a medium pot, put water to boil, add chicken, salt, annatto, and garlic. Leave to boil for 30 minutes. Then add the chocho and coco, and after five minutes add the onions and fresh culantro and boil for another 15 minutes. Then add the oregano and onion leaves and cook for another 15 minutes. Serve with rice or tortillas.

caldo caax

Ixcabeche
Escabeche (S) Onion Soup (E)

1 medium chicken
2-3 L water
2 cloves garlic, crushed
1 tsp black pepper
1 large sweet pepper, sliced
2 carrots, sliced
1 tsp dry oregano, crushed
6 allspice seeds (½ tsp powder)
¼ C lime juice
4 lbs onions, sliced
salt to taste

grilling chicken

Wash the chicken with vinegar or lime juice. Cover the chicken with water in large pot. Add salt and boil for 25 minutes. Remove the chicken and save the water. Grill the chicken over hot coals for 10 minutes on each side until golden brown. Cut into serving size pieces, removing the bones. Set aside.

crushing garlic

making lime juice

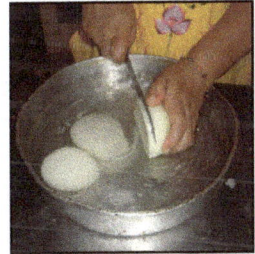

slicing onions

Add garlic, pepper, sweet peppers, carrots, oregano, allspice, some more salt, and lime to the water. Stir. Cut the onions in slices and separate the rings. Add onions and chicken to the soup, stirring for another 15 minutes. Serve with potatoes, rice, or tortillas.

ixcabeche

Boox Janal
Chimole (S) Black Soup (E)

10-12 servings

1 whole medium chicken cut for stew
2 tsp chicken bouillon seasoning
3 cloves garlic
2 large onions, diced
1 T seasoned salt
2 T black recado (¼ of small block)
1 lb potatoes, quartered
1 packet chicken broth soup mix
10-12 eggs
4 medium tomatoes, cut in quarters
1 tsp dry oregano
1 tsp black pepper
1 bunch culantro
2 L water
salt to taste

Wash the chicken with lime or vinegar. Cut the chicken and season with chicken bouillon seasoning, garlic, onions, salt, and seasoned salt. Place in a large pot and simmer covered for 10 minutes. Dissolve the black recado in two liters of water and add the black water to the chicken. Wash and peel the potatoes; cut into four pieces each and add

Boox Janal

to the pot when boiling. Then add soup mix and eggs (with shells). Boil for at least 30 minutes. Add tomatoes, oregano, black pepper, and culantro. Cook another 15 minutes. Prior to serving, remove the shells from the eggs and return the eggs to the soup. Serve with rice, potatoes, or tortillas.

Hot Pepper Sauces and Seasonings

Sa'k Chucan Ik
Su'k Chucan Ik (M) Boiled Peppers (E)

2 habanero peppers (or any hot pepper)
½ C water
pinch of salt

Boil the peppers in water for 15 minutes. Mash well in water and add salt. Serve with game meat, dried or smoked meat, and corn tortillas.

bird peppers

Sa'k Chucan Ik

Ti'kin Juch'an IK
Dried Ground Pepper (E)

1 lb habanero peppers (or any hot pepper)

Put the hot peppers in the sun to dry for several days or dry over the fire on low heat. Grind the dry peppers with a hand mill. Bottle. This is good for two years. Use in wrapped fish, shrimp, conch, lobster, or crab, and also in caldo. Only use a pinch at a time because it is very hot!

Ku'ut Ik
Pu'uchan Ik (M) Peppers with Tomatoes (E)

  2 habanero peppers (or any hot pepper)
  1 large onion, sliced thin
  2 T lime juice
  1 bunch culantro, chopped
  pinch of salt

Roast the peppers and tomatoes for 10 minutes on a comal. Mash the peppers in mortar and pestle. Peel the tomatoes and mash in a mortar and pestle slightly, not completely. Add the onions, lime, salt, and culantro; and mix well. Serve as a side dish with any meal.

roasting peppers and tomatoes

peeling tomatoes

peeled tomatoes

mashing tomatoes

adding tomatoes

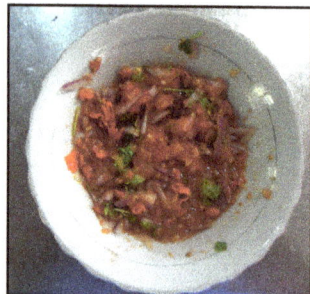
Ku'ut Ik

Tza'jaan Ik Etel Cebolla

Tzu'jaan Ik Etel Cebolla (M)

Fried Peppers with Onions (E)

4 habanero peppers (or any hot pepper)
¼ C water
1 large onion, sliced thin
handful cilantro
1 T oil
pinch of salt

Mash the peppers by hand with a mortar and pestle. Sauté the onions until golden brown. Add the peppers, water, and a pinch of salt. Boil for five minutes. Serve on the dinner table.

slicing onions

sautéing onions

adding peppers

Tza'jaan Ik Etel Cebolla

Pook Bi Ik

Pookaan Ik (M) Roasted Peppers (E)

2 habanero peppers (or any hot pepper)
2 T lime juice
1 medium onion, sliced
1 bunch culantro, diced
pinch of salt

Roast the peppers on a comal for 10 minutes, turning each side. Mash well in a bowl; add salt, lime, culantro, and onions. Serve on the dinner table. Careful, this stuff is hot!

Side Dishes

Waj
Corn Tortillas (E)

12 tortillas

1 lb of masa (p. 14)
1 banana leaf

Moisten the masa, adding water little by little to about the consistency of clay. Form into small balls a little bigger than a cotton ball. With fingers, press the ball of dough on a banana leaf (plastic or foil) and smooth the edges to form tortillas. Pre-heat the comal for 10 minutes before cooking the tortillas. Flip each tortilla when the underside is cooked, but not yet dry on top. If the top dries, moisten with water, then flip. Cook each side for about two minutes. Then flip once more and leave it to puff up by pressing the tortilla against the comal. Wrap in cloth to keep them warm.

| masa balls | tortillas cooking | Waj |

Making tortillas with a press—First cut two round plastic sheets an inch larger than the diameter of the press. Put one plastic sheet on the bottom of the press, place a ball of dough on the plastic, and top with the second sheet of plastic. Lower the top plate and press the dough until 1/8" thick. Remove the plastic, smooth the edges, and place the tortilla on a hot comal to cook.

making tortillas with press

26

Tzi't
Tamalitos (S) Ducano (C)

12 Tamalitos

12 ears of young green corn
1 C oil
12 corn husks
salt to taste

Cut the corn off the cobs. Grind the corn in a hand mill. Mix with oil and salt. Using the largest husks, wrap about two tablespons of the corn mixture into each husk. Put the tamalitos in a pot and fill with water until the they are submerged halfway, but not covered. Boil for about 45 minutes or until the water is gone. Or the tamalitos can be baked in a greased pan at 350°F for one hour.

tzi't witth corn husks removed

Kab'ax Bu'ul
C'ainbil Bu'ul (M) Stew Beans (C)

8 servings

1 medium sweet pepper, chopped
1 lb beans
1 gal water
2 cloves garlic, minced
1 medium onion, sliced
2 T pork fat or oil
salt to taste

Wash the beans thoroughly in a large pot. Add water until the pot is three-fourths full. Cook on high heat for about one hour, adding more water when needed. Add garlic and salt, and cook another hour or until the beans get soft. Sauté the onions in pork fat or oil. Pork fat gives it a better flavor. Add sautéd onions and the sweet peppers to the pot and mix well. Boil for 15 minutes. Serve with tortillas, rice, potatoes, or plantains.

Cha'can Culaj
Chu'can Culaj (M)
Jipijapa Young Shoots (E)

4 servings

  1 lb jipijapa
  1 medium onion, diced
  2 cloves garlic, minced
  2 T oil
  1 small pinch of annatto
  1 C water
  salt to taste

Slice jipijapa into small pieces. Sauté the onions and garlic until golden brown. Add the jipijapa, a cup of water, annatto, and salt and cover. Cook on low heat for about 10 minutes. Serve with rice, tortillas, or potatoes.

slicing jipijapa

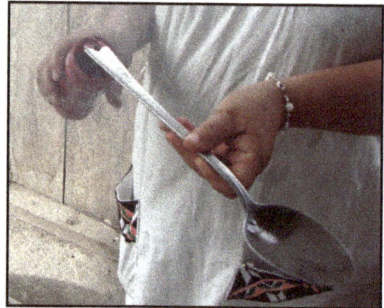
measuring pinch of annatto

adding jipijapa mixture to fry pan

Culaj

Suun Culaj
Jipijapa Pods (E)

4 servings

4 young jipijapa pods
3 gloves garlic, crushed
1 small onion, chopped
1 T oil
1¼ L water
salt to taste

In large pot of water, boil the jipijapa pods in one liter of water for about 30 minutes. Take out the pods. Open them and remove only the hairy part. Throw the rest away. Sauté the onions and garlic. Add the jipijapa, one-quarter cup water, and salt to taste. Cover the pot and cook on low heat until the water is gone, sitrring now and again. Serve with tortillas, rice or potatoes.

Tzayook
Calalloo (S)

6-8 servings

2 lbs calalloo
1 L water
2 T oil
1 large onion, chopped
salt to taste

Put the calalloo and salt in a pot of water. Boil for 30 minutes. Sauté the onions. Strain the calalloo and chop. Put the onions and calalloo in the pot. Cover and shake well. Cook on low heat for five minutes, then serve with a meal.

Tza'haan Ocaro
Tzu'haan Ocaro (M) Fried Okra (E)

6 servings

1 lb fresh okra, sliced
2 T oil
1 medium onion, sliced
6 eggs
salt to taste

Sauté the onions. Add the okra and salt. Cover, lower the heat, and cook for another eight minutes, stirring occasionally. Then crack and add the eggs. Continue stirring until the eggs are cooked. Serve with bread, tortillas, rice, or potatoes.

Tza'haan Ocaro

Cu'ul
Cohune Cabbage (C) Cohune Heart of Palm (E)

16 servings

4 lb cohune heart of palm
4 L water
pinch of annatto
½ C oil
1 large onion, chopped
½ handful of dried oregano
1 tsp black pepper
3 cloves of garlic, crushed
salt to taste

Cut the heart of palm into two-inch cubes. Put it in a pot of water and add salt. Boil until the palm is soft, about three hours. Strain and mash. Sauté the onions. Drop the palm in the fry pan with the onions and add oregano, black pepper, and garlic. Mix a pinch of annatto in a little water and add it to the fry pan. Stir well and cook for 10 minutes. Serve with tortillas, rice, or potates.

Sa'k Chucan Is's
Su'k Chucan Camut (M) Boiled Sweet Potato (E)

4 servings

  1 lb sweet potatoes
  1T brown sugar
  2 C water

Peel the potatoes and cut into small cubes. Boil them in water for 15 minutes and add sugar. Stir and boil for another 30 minutes. Serve alone or with a meal.

Tza'haan Is's
Tzu'haan Camut (M) Fried Sweet Potato (E)

6 servings

  2 lb sweet potatoes
  1 C oil
  salt to taste

Peel and slice the potatoes in rounds about one-quarter inch thick. Add a pinch of salt to each slice. Heat the oil and cook on each side for five minutes. Serve alone or with a meal.

Pi' Ris 'Pak
Boiled Tomatoes in Eggs (E)

4 servings

  1 lb tomatoes
  5 eggs
  1 large onion, diced
  1 bunch culantro, finely chopped
  ¾ L water
  salt to taste

Culaj

Bring water to boil. Add the eggs in their shells and tomatoes. Boil for 15 minutes and remove the contents, setting the water aside for later. Peel the boiled tomatoes and chop finely. Peel the eggs and slice into rounds. Add salt, onions, and culantro. Mix together with a couple tablespoons of left over water to moisten. Serve with bread or tortillas.

Yax Tzu'haan Jaaz
Mun Tzu'jaan Jaaz (M) Green Plantain (E)

4 servings

4 green plantains
or 6 green bananas
½ L water
1 lb pigtail, game or dried meat
¼ tsp black pepper
1 garlic clove, crushed
1 tsp chicken bouillon
¼ C oil
1 medium onion, chopped
1 sweet pepper
salt to taste

green plantains

Peel the plantains and boil in salted water for 15 minutes. Add the pigtail, black pepper, garlic, and chicken bouillon. Sauté the onion and add onion and sweet pepper to the pot. Mix well and boil for 30 minutes and serve hot.

Optional
4 pieces fish

Season the fish with salt and black pepper. Fry the fish. Add to the top of the plantain mixture 15 minutes before the plantains are done. Do not mix.

Mun Tzii'haan Jaaz
Plantain Chips (E)

2 servings

1 large plantain
1 C oil
pinch of salt

Peel the plantain and slice in rounds like coins. Add salt. Heat the oil in a fry pan and add the plantain, turning now and again for almost 20 minutes or until golden brown. Eat by itself or with any meat or beans.

Sa'k Chucan Jaaz
Su'k Chucan Jaaz (M) Boiled Ripe Plantain (E)

6 servings

2 ripe medium plantains
1 C water
1 T oil

Peel the plantains and cut into halves, then cut lengthwise. Boil in water for 15 minutes. Before cutting off the heat, add oil. Serve as a side dish or eat alone.

Tzi'haan Jaaz
Baked Plantain (C)

6 servings

2 ripe plantains
2 C oil

Peel the plantains and cut into halves, and then cut lengthwise. Heat oil and fry in low heat, flipping them now and again. Cook for 15 minutes. Serve with any meal or rice and beans.

Ti'kaan Jaaz
Ka'kaan Jaaz (M) Baked Ripe Plantain (E)

2 servings

2 overripe plantains
2 T margarine or butter
2 pieces of foil

Peel the plantains and cut into them lengthwise, but not completely. Add margarine or butter inside the plantain, one tablespoon each. Wrap tightly in foil and put on a baking sheet. Bake for about 30 minutes at 350°. Serve alone or with a meal.

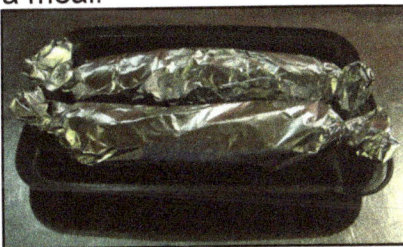

peeled plantains ready to bake

Ti'kaan Jaaz

33

Tzi'haan Jaaz
Fried Plantain (C)

6 servings

2 ripe plantains
1 C oil

Peel the plantains and cut into strips about one inch thick. Heat oil and fry plantains, turning them when underneath turns golden brown. Cook about four minutes on each side. Serve with food, such as, rice and beans.

Pook Bi Jaaz
Pookaan Jaaz (M) Roasted Ripe Plantain (E)

2 servings

2 overripe plantains
2 tsp margarine or butter

Cook over a grill or on coals with peel intact. Turn once in a while for about 30 minutes. Cut through the peel. Add margarine or butter. Scoop out the plantain with a spoon. Serve alone or with a meal.

roasting

peeling plantains

Pook Bi Jaaz

Ku'ut Tzu'haan Jaaz
Pu'uchan Tzu'jaan Jaaz (M)
Mashed Ripe Plantain (E)

6 servings

2 overripe plantains
1 C coconut oil

Peel and mash the plantains. Heat the oil and add the mashed plantains. Turn them continually until cooked completely, about 15 minutes. Serve with any dish.

34

Main Dishes

Ixpa' Cha Miziim
P'axjaan Miziim (M) Steamed Shrimp (E)

3-4 servings

    1 lb shrimp (fish, or crab)
    2 obel leaves, torn into pieces
    1 fresh banana leaf
    salt to taste
    optional: dried hot pepper powder

Soak the shrimp in boiling water, drain the water, then peel the shrimp. Mix the shrimp, obel and salt. Wrap all in a banana leaf. Cook for 60 minutes on a grill and turn after 30 minutes. Serve with tortillas or rice.

Alternate method of cooking: Wrap with foil. Bake in oven for 45 minutes at 350°F, flipping after 22 minutes.

ingredients on banana leaf

wrapping

on the grill

ixpa' cha miziim

Cha'caan Qe Qun
Tzu'haan Eq'en (M) Maya Pork Stew (E)

8 servings

2 lb pork
1 pinch of annatto
1 tsp black pepper
1 tsp cumin
3 garlic cloves, crushed
1 large onion, chopped
1 tsp pork broth
2 C water
1 handful dried oregano
15 leaves fresh culantro
1 bunch green onion leaves
salt to taste

Wash the pork and cut into serving size pieces. Mix the pork with annatto, salt, black pepper, cumin, garlic, onions, and pork broth. Put in medium pot, cover and cook on low heat for 15 minutes. Add water and boil for another 15 minutes. Add oregano and culantro and boil for 20 minutes. Add onion leaves and simmer for 10 minutes, adding more water if necessary. Serve with tortillas or rice.

cha' caan qe qun

Cha'caan Caax
Tzu'haan Caax (M) Mayan Stewed Chicken (E)

8 servings

1 medium chicken
1 medium onion, chopped
1 tsp black pepper
3 cloves garlic, crushed
1 T oil
1 pinch of annatto
1 tsp oregano
1 bunch of culantro
salt to taste

cha'caan caax

Wash the chicken and cut into serving size pieces. Sauté the onions. Mix the chicken with all ingredients, except oregano and culantro. Put in a medium pot, cover, and cook on low heat for 10 minutes. Then add water and boil for 30 minutes, stirring occasionally. Add oregano, stir and cook for 15 minutes. Add culantro, stir and cook for another 15 minutes. Serve with tortillas, rice, or potatoes.

Ka'kaan Caax
Baked Chicken (E)

8-10 servings

1 medium chicken
1 large onion, chopped
2 cloves garlic, crushed
1 tsp chicken bouillon
1 tsp seasoned salt
3 T barbeque sauce
1 tsp red recado, dissolved in water
3 T butter
salt to taste

Wash and cut the chicken into serving size pieces. Season with all ingredients except butter. Spread on a baking sheet, putting the butter on top. Cover with foil and bake for 45 minutes at 350°F. Serve with tortillas, rice, or potatoes.

Bollos
Tamales (S)

12 Bollos

2 banana leaves

Roast the leaves directly over a fire or burner on both sides to soften. Cut each leaf into six pieces, three pieces on each side of the vein. Sponge each piece with a damp cloth and set aside. Save the veins for later.

Red filling:
½ tsp black pepper
¼ tsp annatto
1 tsp chicken bouillon
1 medium onion, chopped
1 clove garlic, crushed
1 T oil
½ lb masa (p.14)
1 C water
salt to taste

In a medium pot, mix the salt, pepepr, annatto, bouillon, onion, garlic, and oil. Add the masa and water. Bring to a boil, stirring constantly. Remove when boiling. Set aside.

Tamale base:
1½ lbs masa
¾ C oil
some water
salt to taste

Mix the masa with the oil, adding water until it is as soft as clay. Form into 12 balls. Place each ball on a piece of banana leaf. Flatten each ball into a tortilla shape.

Add one teaspoon of the red filling to the center of each open tamale.

Chicken tamales: Cook two legs of chicken and cut each leg into six pieces of meat. Add one piece of meat to each tamale.

Vegetarian tamales: Substitute vegetable boullion for chicken bouillon and add cooked greens or heart of palm.

38

Fold the masa over the filling, one side and then the other. Next, fold the banana leaf over the tamale lengthwise and on the ends. Put the banana leaf veins on the bottom of the pot. Place the tamales on top of the veins, add water, but do not completely cover the tamales, and boil for one hour.

Bollos

Tamal

Many varieties of tamales exist in Central America. In the Yucatec and Mopan cultures the Tamal differs from the Bollos in several ways. For a Tamal, the corn is cooked for 30 minutes and then sieved finely. Oil and salt are added. It is then cooked slowly to thicken, stirring constantly, at least 30 minutes. Instead of wrapping the filling in the masa, the meat is laid on top of the masa and pushed into it, along with culantro, mint, and basil. An annatto drip is sprinkled on top of the masa. The piece of banana leaf is folded over the masa and meat

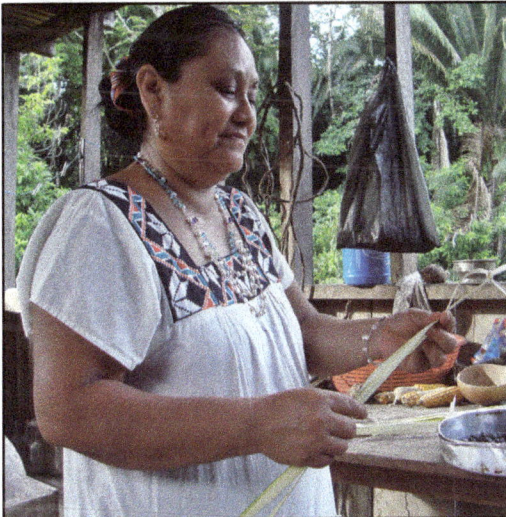

making ties from jipijapa young shoots

lengthwise and on the ends. In addition, a Tamal is tied with leaves from the young shoots of the jipijapa that have been separated and torn in half lengthwise. As with Bollos, Tamal are boiled for about an hour in a pot with banana leaf veins in the bottom and water that does not cover.

Desserts

Ka'kaan Jaaz
Baked Plantain Cake (E)

8 servings

6 overripe plantains
½ C margarine or butter
½ C brown sugar
¼ C flour
1 T vanilla
½ tsp baking powder

Peel, slice, and mash the plantains. Soften the margarine or butter over the fire and mix all the ingredients. Spread into a greased baking pan and bake for 45 minutes at 250°F until golden brown on the top or by testing with a toothpick.

slicing plantains

mashing plantains

measuring vanilla

ka'kaan jaaz

Chu'huk Zum
Chu'huk Chum (M) Chocho (C) Chayote (S)

6 servings

4 medium young chocho
½ lb brown sugar
1 L water

Wash the chocho and slice each into five slices. In a medium pot, add sugar, chocho slices, and water. Boil for 45 minutes. Serve as a dessert.

chu'hhuk zum

Chu'huk C'um
Ayote Conserva (S) Stewed Pumpkin (E)

6 servings

1 medium pumpkin
1 lb brown sugar
1½ L water

Wash the pumpkin, remove the seeds, and cut into two-inch cubes. Boil in water for 15 minutes. Add sugar and boil for 60 minutes. Serve as a dessert. This dish is traditionally prepared at Christmas.

cho'c'um

Tz'yan Arroz
Rice Lab (E)

6 servings

½ lb rice
1½ L water
1 tin sweetened
    condensed milk
1tsp cinnamon

Fresh rice just harvested or brown rice works best to make lab. Wash the rice and boil in water for half hour. Add condensed milk, cinnamon, and mix well.

Tz'yan Arroz

Maja Blanca
Rice Pudding (E)

10 servings

½ lb rice
2 L water

Soak the rice overnight. Strain and wash the rice with cold water. Grind in a matate. Put in a pot, add water, stir, and cook over low heat until it thickens. Add sugar and milk to taste. Serve with cinnamon on top.

Chu'huk Waj
Corn Biscuit (E)

20 biscuits

½ lbl corn
1 C oil

Prepare the corn as for masa. Wash off the skin and drain through a hanging cloth overnight to dry. The next morning grind very fine in a matate. Mix with sugar to taste and oil. Knead to form a dough the consistency of clay. Make small balls and flatten like a tortilla as thin as possible. Decorate like making a hole in the middle, zigzag along the edge or pressing the shape of a flower. Heat the comal to low heat. Cook until golden brown on both sides.

Index

Authors

Aurora Garcia Saqui, artist, herbalist and Mayan activist, was born into a farming family in the village of San Antonio, Cayo District, Belize. One day, while doing her chores, she came across a piece of slate and had the idea to carve and etch the figure of a whale. Her inspiration resurrected an ancient Maya custom and became a family business when she and her sisters created the Garcia Sisters Art Gallery and Museum. They have received national and international recognition in magazines and travel guides for their slate carvings. An innovative artist, Aurora also produces clay masks, basketry, fine jewelry and other crafts.

While Aurora focused on her art, her great uncle, the famed healer Don Elijio Panti, encouraged her to become his apprentice and over thirteen years he conveyed his vast knowledge of the medicinal plants of Belize. Just before he died, he bestowed upon her the responsibility to carry on in his footsteps. Furthermore, he told her that whatever she learned she must teach her own people. Aurora has a four-acre botanical garden and medicine trail. She offers Mayan spiritual blessings, prayer healings, acupuncture, massage, and homemade herbal remedies at her clinic, the Hmen Herbal Center.

An activist for Mayan heritage, Aurora is committed to promoting cultural traditions through presentations, including cooking demonstrations, seminars on herbal medicine, and ceremonial rituals. She and her family accommodate guests and operate the gift shop at Nu'uk Che'il Cottages in the village of Maya Centre and welcome your visit <http://nuukcheilcottages.com>. If you are interested in scheduling Aurora for your group or event, she can be contacted at <nuukcheil@yahoo.com> or phone +501-665-1313/+501-670-7043.

Amy Lichty, renewal coach and consultant, helps individuals and organizations engage in life with purpose and meaning. When she moved to Belize, she became interested in Mayan culture and traditional healing practices. This cookbook has given her the opportunity to understand how essential it is to sustain cultural traditions for future generations. She is grateful for the friendship Aurora and her family have extended to her. She can be contacted at <amy.lichty@dreamweaversinstitute.com>.

www.ingramcontent.com/pod-product-compliance
Lightning Source LLC
Chambersburg PA
CBHW070033110426
42741CB00035B/2760